CREATION OF HEAVEN, EARTH, *and* MAN

OUR STORY

JAMYE R

Literary Illustrations Creative Media Group LLC.
Detroit, MI
https://www.licmediagroup.com

All rights reserved. No part of this book may be reproduced or used in any manner without the prior written permission of the copyright owner, except for the use of brief quotations in a book review.

To request permissions, contact the publisher at info@licfiction.com

Paperback: 978-1-953046-13-0
eBook: 978-1-953046-14-7

First paperback edition 09012022

Edited by Jamye R
Book Cover Design by Literary Illustrations Creative Media Group
Layout by Tialie Simpson

Copyright © 2022 Jamye R.

CONTENTS

God is Triune; Father, Son, Holy Spirit. 1
    Who is God the Father? 1
    Who is God the Son (Son of God)? 2
    God the Holy Spirit 4

Man is also a Triune Being Spirit, Soul, Body. 7
    The Spirit of Man 7
    The Soul of Man 8
    The Body of Man 8

Heaven and Earth 11

Man Was Created for Relationships 17

Deceived by a Serpent 21

Man's Effort To Cover His Sin 27

God's Response to Man's Sin 29

Sin Has Consequences 31

God's Grace, Mercy and Love 37

The Gift of God 41

References 47

GOD IS TRIUNE; FATHER, SON, HOLY SPIRIT

Who is God the Father?

God the Father is the creator of all things. The Father of all creation; He commanded the entire universe to come into existence. Everything was created out of nothing. Genesis 1:1 says, "In the beginning, God created the heavens and the earth."

This means that He was the creator of the world and everything in it. He is the Father of the universe and creation. God is the source of life.

It is through these truths of a relationship with our creator that God is seen as Father over all. The Bible also tells us that God was the literal Father of Jesus.

And that Jesus was His one and only Son. "For God so loved the world, that He gave His one and only Son, that whoever believes in Him should not perish but have eternal life." **John 3:16**

Who is God the Son (Son of God)?

Many theologians and religions argue about if Jesus is God. Some said He was a prophet; a teacher and some religions strangely claim He was a god but not God. Let's take a look in the Bible and see what the scriptures say. In John 1:1-2, 14 we read, In the beginning was the Word, and the Word was with God, and the Word was God. He was in the beginning with God... And the Word became flesh and dwelt among us, and we have seen his glory, glory as of the only Son from the Father, full of grace and truth.

When we read, "In the beginning was the Word" in John's Gospel, we should immediately think of another Bible text that begins with the same introductory phrase. Genesis 1:1 says, "In the beginning, God created the heavens and the earth." Here we can see that Jesus was there in the beginning and He was with and was God.

The Old Testament attests that only God has the power to forgive sins. In **Isaiah 43:25** God says, "I, I am He who blots out your transgressions for My own sake, and I will not remember your sins." It is the Lord who grants mercy and forgiveness.

Therefore, it would have been blasphemy for anyone to claim to be able to forgive sins. This knowledge sheds light on several instances in the Gospels where Jesus claims His Sonship as part of the Godhead. One such remarkable moment is when four men lowered their paralyzed friend through a roof.

As told in **Mark 2:5-12**: "And when Jesus saw their faith, He said to the paralytic, "Son, your sins are forgiven." Now some of the scribes were sitting there, questioning in their hearts. "Why does this man speak like that? He is blaspheming! Who can forgive sins but God alone?" And immediately Jesus, perceiving in His spirit that they thus questioned within themselves, said to them, "Why do you question these things in your hearts? Which is easier, to say to the paralytic, your sins are forgiven, or to say, Rise, take up your bed and walk?"

But that you may know that the Son of Man has authority on earth to forgive sins. He said to the paralytic "I say to you, rise, pick up your bed, and go home." And he rose and immediately picked up his bed and went out before them all, so that they were all amazed and glorified God, saying, "We never saw anything like this!" Now the scribes were not wrong when they mentioned that only God can forgive sins.

By forgiving the paralytic of his sins, Jesus was claiming His place in the Godhead as the Son of God. He healed the man of paralysis to prove the man's sins had been forgiven to those around them, and the witnesses glorified God because of it.

Colossians chapter 1 is mostly focused on describing Christ as supreme. Jesus is not only the God of creation; He is the ultimate authority over all created things. In verses 16 and 17 it states "For by Him were all things created, that are in heaven, and that are in earth, visible and invisible, whether they be thrones, or dominions, or principalities, or powers: all things were created by Him, and for him. And He is before all things, and by Him all things consist." After referring to the scriptures we can conclude with confidence that Jesus is not just the Son of God. He is in fact God.

God the Holy Spirit

Along with God the Father and God the Son (Jesus Christ), God the Spirit is the third member of the Godhead. The **Holy Spirit** as described in the Bible is fully God.

One of the most convincing statements in the Bible about the Holy Spirit being God is found in **Acts 5** when Ananias lied about the price of a piece of property. Peter said that Satan had filled Ananias's heart to "lie to the Holy Spirit" (**Acts 5:3**) and concluded by saying that Ananias had "lied to God" (verse 4). Peter's words equate the Holy Spirit is with God; he spoke as if the Spirit and God were one and the same.

The Bible also displays the Holy Spirit as a person that has a mind, feelings and emotions. He can be grieved (**Ephesians 4:30**), and He has a will (**1 Corinthians 12:4-7**). He is God within us and an active God among us.

The Holy Spirit speaks within many prophets and reveals all the plans and purposes of God. The Spirit is an instructor to ministers and is our counselor. One taught by the Holy Spirit knows the will of God.

He connects us and helps us find God within us. Our body is the temple of the Holy Spirit. We have everything we need with the Holy Spirit in our hearts and the scriptures in our hands.

As a believer He is the most valuable asset to have. He is in charge of Gods affairs on the earth realm. The Holy Spirit is continuing the work that Jesus begun.

Jesus told His disciples that the Holy Spirit, the Helper, was different from Himself. The Father would send the Helper, the Spirit of truth, after Christ departed. What we do know is that there is only one God and that Jesus is God, the Father is God, and the Holy Spirit is God.

MAN IS ALSO A TRIUNE BEING SPIRIT, SOUL, BODY

The Spirit of Man

It's the part of man that was created to commune with God (God Consciousness), man was created to worship God and have fellowship with his creator. In order to contact or worship God, who is Spirit, we must use our spirit. The spirit in man is God's breath which gives man life both physically and spiritually. (Gen 2:7)

When God's breathe is removed from man he dies physically. (Ecclesiastes 3:19-21, Ecclesiastes 12:7) Spiritually; the spirit of man connects us to the spirit of God, giving hope to man awakening him to the awareness of God, bringing man into living life as God intended for man to live. (Job 32:8, Job 33:4, Hebrews 4:12) Our human spirit is so important to

God because **God wants to fill us with Himself**. He wants us to receive Him, and our spirit is the unique receiver.

The Soul of Man

The soul is our very self, a medium between our spirit and our body, possessing self-consciousness. Our soul is our personality of who we are. It's the part of man that gives him the ability to think and store thoughts, knowledge and memories.

The mind dwells in the soul and our soul is housed in our hearts. Therefore, contrary to popular belief our mind is in our heart not in our brain. The soul has feelings and develops emotions. With our soul we think, reason, consider, remember, and wonder. We experience emotions like happiness, love, sorrow, anger, relief, and compassion. And we're able to resolve, choose, and make decisions. (Psalms 23:3, Psalms 35:9, Psalms 139:14, Matt 10:28

The Body of Man

Our body exists in and contacts the tangible things of the material world using our five physical senses. The body is the visible, external part of our being, and it contains the soul. Our soul is the vessel containing our spirit. It's the part of man that is flesh and was formed from the dust of the ground.

The body is the physical host of the spirit and soul. As well as the temple of the Holy Spirit that is in us which we received from God. It is also a member of Christ; it is not our own. Without God's breathe the body will perish. (Gen 2:7, 1 Cor 6:12-2) In the spirit, God as the Spirit dwells; in the soul, our self-dwells; and in the body, the physical senses dwell.

God sanctifies us, first, by taking possession of our spirit through regeneration (John 3:5-6); second, by spreading Himself as the life-giving Spirit from our spirit into our soul to saturate and transform our soul (Rom. 12:2; 2 Cor. 3:18); and last, by enlivening our mortal body through our soul (Rom. 8:11, 13) and transfiguring our body by His life power (Phil. 3:21)."

HEAVEN AND EARTH

In Genesis it gives a narrative account on the creation of the heavens, earth and all living things including man. In the beginning God created the heavens and the earth. The earth was covered with water. It probably had the appearance of mud, with no dry land and no breathable atmosphere.

Its entire surface was liquid elements, predominantly water, situated in a spherical shape and hung on nothing in space (**Job 26:7**). Also covering the earth were heavy, thick clouds, fog, and mist, all of which engulfed the earth in pitch black darkness (**Genesis 2:4-6**, esp. **Genesis 2:6**).

On the first **day of creation**, God said, "Let there be light" (**Genesis 1:3**), and light appeared as a thing separate from darkness. The phrase let there be light is a translation of the Hebrew phrase yehi 'or, which was translated "fiat lux" in Latin. A literal translation would be a command, something like "Light, exist." God is speaking into the void and commanding light to come into being.

The Bible tells us that God created the heavens and the earth and everything else that exists by simply speaking them into existence (**Genesis 1**). His personality, power, creativity, and beauty were expressed in creation the same way an artist's personality and personal attributes are expressed through art or music.

The idea of light, existing first in God's mind, was given form by the words "Let there be light" or "Let light exist." The reality of the creative power of God's voice has important spiritual implications that go well beyond the creation account itself.

Now, the second day of creation takes place. God is ready to divide the waters and to create the physical laws that will cause the clouds, fog, and mist to leave the face of the earth and rise up and hang in the sky above the earth.

The dividing or separating of the waters created what we'd call an atmosphere within the chaos of the watery universe.

On following days God gathered the lower waters and caused dry land to appear and burst with vegetation, and he created lights in the dome of the sky, sea life and birds, and creatures on the land. But life was predicated on keeping chaos at bay, keeping the upper and lower waters, which were always threatening to break through in their place. God accomplished this by means of the firmament, the hard, hammered-out dome of the sky. The firmament described here is the overlay that divided the waters below from the waters above is the first heaven.

God brought the world into existence and as the capstone of this good work, He created people in His image so that they could share in His overflowing love, grace and goodness through their relationships with God and man.

God did not need the world or need people because God has no lack.

God created people to reflect His image, to rule over creation, and to reproduce godly offspring. God decrees, "Let us make man in our image," using a Hebrew word—ē'nu—which is unmistakably plural. Why does God speak of Himself as more than one person? Scholars have offered a wide variety of ideas over the centuries. Three explanations are offered more often than any others.

First, God may be referring to Himself and the angels. This seems unlikely given the rest of Scripture's depiction of angels. These beings are presented as servants and messengers, not creators or rulers. Second, this could be what scholars call a plural of self-exhortation or self-encouragement, meaning He is referring only to Himself. This would also be referred to as "the royal" something we see used by human kings and rulers when making proclamations or decrees.

The third possibility is that God is speaking as a Trinity, of Father, Son, and Holy Spirit. According to Scripture as a whole, the full Trinity was present at creation. Genesis 1:2 describes the Spirit of God hovering over the waters, and John 1:1–3 reveals that the Word, Christ, was active in the creation of all things.

What does it mean to be made in God's image, or in His likeness? Without question, this statement does not mean that God created humans to resemble Him physically (John 4:24). Rather, this seems to support the idea that God endowed humans with a certain kind of awareness, one which animals and birds and fish were not given.

In other words, humans would possess the capacity for reason, morality, language, personality, and purpose. In particular, the ability to use morality and spirituality are unique to human beings among God's creations on earth. Like God, we would possess the capacity to experience and understand love, truth, and beauty.

Humans are made in God's image in another way: as a model, or a representative. God is the Maker, and all of creation belongs to Him. He is Lord over it. However, in the moment of creation, God gives mankind the responsibility to rule over all other life He has made on the earth. In that sense, humans would stand as God's image, God's representatives, on earth as we rule over and manage all the rest of His creation.

MAN WAS CREATED FOR RELATIONSHIPS

The very first relationship man had was with his creator. God the Most High came down to earth and communicated with Adam often. They had a fellowship amongst each other, they were friends. God loved Adam and loves us; He cares about our thoughts and asked our opinion. God brought every animal and bird to Adam to see what he would call them. Whatever Adam called it became its name. (Gen 2:15, 19-20)

The second relationship was with another human being. God noticed that it was not good for man to be alone. He decided to make man a helper, one that is comparable to him. This companion will be suitable for man, a perfect fit to make a special union. This person will have certain characteristics which man would need and each would fit perfectly into the other, complimenting each other. (Gen 2:18)

How did God get this second person for Adam? He did it in a very unique way. God performed the first surgery. He put Adam in a deep sleep and took a part of man out of him and put it within this second person. Man is now incomplete without this other person. And this other person will not be whole without man. (Gen 2:21)

After God created this second person for Adam, we can see in scripture that God did not just leave her somewhere in the garden for Adam to find. But God Himself brought her to Adam, (God was her Father giver). What was Adam's reaction when he saw her? He was satisfied and Adam named her "woman". His reasoning was that she was taken out of man. Woman was created to provide man with whatever he was lacking. (Gen 2:23)

Then God our Father gave her to Adam and performed the first marriage ceremony, making man and woman into one union. Therefore, a man should leave his father and mother to be joined with his wife and a father should give his daughter to be joined with her husband, and they shall become one flesh. And they both were naked, the man and his wife, and they were not ashamed.

Sex is permissible between a husband and wife, a wedding gift from God. This sexual union does have its effects; it ties the two souls together every time. God has given sex to us as a means of glorifying Him as we fulfill its design for procreation, intimacy, comfort, and physical pleasure. It is a fulfillment of God's created order in marriage between a husband and wife. (Gen 2:24-25)

DECEIVED BY
A SERPENT

Who was this serpent? What was his special characteristic that made him stand out from the rest of the beasts? We learned from the bible that the serpent was a very attractive, appealing and quaint animal. The serpent was more cunning than any other beast on the land. He had certain mannerisms and movements that brought attention to him. Adam and his wife were most likely mesmerized by this serpent. At this time, the serpent apparently was able to walk upright. (Gen 3:1)

One day the serpent spoke. "A talking serpent?" "What did he say?" we might wonder. The answer can be found in Genesis 3:1-5. Furthermore, why would this serpent talk about God in this manner? Or was it actually someone else speaking these things?

Keep in mind that demons are constantly observing everything we do to find an opportunity to attack us. Once they gain this knowledge about us, they just wait on the perfect time to strike. Satan knew that the woman admired this creature. He took advantage of that and used the serpent to deceive her.

Now, this conversation between the woman and the serpent was much more than just mere words. It caused detrimental hardships to the man and woman. But first let's consider how accurate was this conversation?

What did God say? (Gen 2:16-17)

Compare what God said to what the serpent is trying to get the woman to believe. First the serpent began this conversation with a question. "Has God said you shall not eat of every tree of the garden?" His motive as we would see later is to get her to question the validity of God's word and to cause her to disbelieve what God said.

How did the woman answer the serpent's question? (Gen 3:2-3)

What did she add that God did not say? (Gen 3:3)

We read in the scriptures that she added "nor shall you touch it" because the serpent was playing with her mind. God would have not allowed any error.

Now the serpent moved in with his agenda which was to put unbelief of the word of God in the soul or heart of the woman. In Genesis 3:4-5, he said "you will not surely die." He was making God out to be a liar, causing her to distrust God and to believe the serpent.

He continues in verse 5, "For God knows that in the day you eat of it your eyes will be opened, and you will be like God, knowing good and evil." In other words, the serpent is telling the woman that she needs and can obtain knowledge on her own. And in order to get it she has to get as far as she can away from God, go about it on her own and do whatever she has to do to get it.

Who is this character using the voice of a simple beast called "serpent" to speak to the woman? (Gen 3:1-5) The answer can be found in several passages; Isaiah 14:12-17, Luke 10:17-18, Revelation 12:9, Revelation 20:2&10, 2 Corinthians 11:3

Where did this character or personality (Satan) come from; what was his origin?

Ezekiel 28:12-17

12 "Son of man, raise a funeral song over the king of Tyre. Tell him, A Message from God, the Master: "You had everything going for you.

13 You were in Eden, God's garden. You were dressed in splendor, your robe studded with jewels: Carnelian, peridot, and moonstone, beryl, onyx, and jasper, Sapphire, turquoise, and emerald, all in settings of engraved gold. A robe was prepared for you the same day you were created.

14 You were the anointed cherub. I placed you on the mountain of God. You strolled in magnificence among the stones of fire.

15 From the day of your creation you were sheer perfection... and then imperfection - evil! - was detected in you.

16 In much buying and selling you turned violent, you sinned! I threw you, disgraced, off the mountain of God. I threw you out - you, the anointed angel-cherub. No more strolling among the gems of fire for you!

17 Your beauty went to your head. You corrupted wisdom by using it to get worldly fame. I threw you to the ground, sent you sprawling before an audience of kings and let them gloat over your demise.

What good would this conversation bring Satan (serpent) if his words are believed and followed by the man and his wife?

The serpent made the woman believe that she

would be equal to God knowing everything He

knows, she would be like God. He caused her to

distrust God and this is where the root of man's distrust in God developed. Furthermore, the woman saw this tree and looked at it every day, but now it became a lust or a longing for. Satan wanted what God had given to Adam which was dominion and ruler ship over the earth. This was an opportunity for him steal it.

Compare Genesis 1:26-28 with 2 Corinthians 4:4 – In 2 Corinthians 4:4 we see Satan being called the god of this age. He is not the god of the earth; he did not form it but rather he is the god or originator of the current world system. 1 John 2:16 says "For all that is in the world – the lust of the flesh, the lust of the eyes, and the pride of life – is not of the Father but is of the world." (The Father referenced here is the Most High, God the Father) Satan's ultimate desire is to be like God. Satan wants to be worshipped. (John 12:31 John 14:30 John 17:15)

MAN'S EFFORT TO COVER HIS SIN

What effects did eating the forbidden fruit have on Adam and his wife? (Gen 3:6-10)

Their eyes were opened to their sin (wrongdoing) and they knew that they had done wrong. They saw more than their physical nakedness. This awareness was of the soul. Their conscience was awakened, and they knew that they were not the same. Something within them had changed; they felt ashamed and had to hide. But what were they hiding from? They were trying to hide from the light. God is light and light exposes; causes exposure. (1 John 1:5 John 3:19-21)

Can anyone hide from the presence of God? (Psalms 139:1-3, 7)

Man attempted to cover his inner (soul) nakedness with fig leaves. From the time that he was created man had always been in fellowship with his creator.

It even continued after God had given man a wife. He would fellowship with the couple quite often while they were naked, and they were never ashamed to be in God's presence prior. So, what is this nakedness they are trying to cover all of a sudden? Was it their effort to cover the shame they were feeling within? They now feared the One who created and loved them and hid from Him. (Gen 3:10)

GOD'S RESPONSE TO MAN'S SIN

God went in search of man and his wife, not that He was not aware of their whereabouts. God was reaching out to man even after they disobeyed Him. God called out to man asking; Where are you? The man replied that he was hiding because he was naked.

God continued to question man. Who told you that you were naked? Have you eaten from the tree of which I commanded you that you should not eat? Now of course God knew the answers to these questions, nevertheless He continued to question man in attempt to get him to confess, admit and accept responsibility of his wrong doing. God did not want to condemn man, He just needed man to acknowledge and repent for his actions.

The definition of repent is to change the mind. Repentance is the activity of confessing one's actions and feeling regret for past wrong doings, along with actual actions to prove commitment to change and do better. Man did not want to repent and own up to what he did. He replied to God; 'The woman who you gave to be with me, she gave me of the tree and I ate."

Here we see that man was blaming God for what he had done because it was God that gave him the wife whom influenced him. When God confronted woman about what she had done she immediately blamed the serpent. Through blame Adam gave his authority to Eve by blaming her for him eating the forbidden fruit. This is how the "Feminine Movement" was birth. However, Eve gave the authority to Satan by blaming the serpent for her actions. This is how Satan stole our power of dominion over the earth.

SIN HAS CONSEQUENCES

After a quick interrogation, God determines the guilt of all involved, and issues curses upon them in the order the offenses were committed—on the serpent, the woman, and the man. In Genesis 3:14 God was speaking to the physical serpent, the beast. In verse 15, He spoke to the spiritual serpent, Satan; we will explore this verse more. In verse 16 God addressed Eve;

> To the woman He said,
> "I will greatly multiply
> Your pain in childbirth,
> In pain you will bring forth children;
> Yet your desire will be for your husband,
> And he will rule over you."

For the woman, she would experience great pain during labor and delivery of children. Yet it gets interesting when it comes to her husband. The word "desire" means craving or longing. The issue is we make the substitution of God for a husband. A woman desire should be for God. Instead, her desire, craving, longing is misplaced.

The problem is that they exalt the men in their lives and look to them for affirmation and provision emotionally and spiritually for things that God alone is supposed to provide. They looked to men to meet a need they couldn't meet; emotionally, spiritually, physically. This unquenchable craving is an issue of worship and idolatry.

Besides Christ, their inclination after the fall is to set up men as being able to meet needs in them that only God can meet, and there is no limit to how desperate we can become. And instead of acknowledging our sovereign, understanding, and knowledgeable Father in heaven as the place to which they should have looked, they started looking within themselves once the men in their lives disappointed them.

Then finally he said to Adam in Genesis 3:17-19; "Because you listened to your wife and ate fruit from the tree about which I commanded you, 'You must not eat from it, "Cursed is the ground because of you; through painful toil you will eat food from it all the days of your life. It will produce thorns and thistles for you, and you will eat the plants of the field. By the sweat of your brow you will eat your food until you return to the ground, since from it you were taken; for dust you are and to dust you will return."

Adam's sin goes deeper than just listening to his wife and eating of the forbidden fruit. He sinned by not standing up and bringing correction to his wife when she lured him to engage in her act. Also, he did not protect Eve against the serpent and guide her away from him as a husband should. Most importantly he did not heed to God's word, adhere to His godly counsel and spiritually lead his wife.

God held Adam accountable independently for his actions and his choice to eat from the tree. He was not going to be able to pass the blame on Eve or anyone else, including God.

In the same degree as with woman, man's curse is one of hardship in performing the essential duties of life. Before the fall doing these things were joyful and had a substantial meaning. Due to the ground now being cursed man's once light workload became burdensome labor.

Man will suffer from inevitable sorrow in getting the ground to produce edible food. And this curse will afflict him all the days of his life. Let's take account and reflect on that woman's curse involves pain and struggle in family relationships, while man's bring pain and frustration in working life.

We call this episode in human history the fall of man because, in that act of disobedience, Adam brought a curse upon every person yet to be born. One of the immediate effects of the Fall was that mankind was separated from God.

In the Garden of Eden, Adam and Eve had perfect communion and fellowship with God. The man who was designed to walk with God in unbroken fellowship had fallen from that exalted position. When they rebelled against Him, that fellowship was broken.

Man was doomed to live in a broken state, in a broken world, apart from ongoing communion with a holy God. They became aware of their sin and were ashamed before Him. They hid from Him, and man has been hiding from God ever since.

Only through Christ can that fellowship be restored, because in Him we are made as righteous and sinless in God's eyes as Adam and Eve were before they sinned. "God made Him who had no sin to be sin for us, so that in Him we might become the righteousness of God." God promised that the **Seed of the woman** would one day save them from the eternal consequences of their sin, but the temporary earthly consequences of sin remained.

Because of the Fall, death became a reality, and all creation was subject to it. All men die, all animals die, all plant life dies. The "whole creation groans", waiting for the time when

Christ will return to free it from the effects of death. Because of sin, death is an inescapable reality, and no one is immune.

"For the wages of sin is death, but the gift of God is eternal life in Christ Jesus our Lord". Worse still, we not only die, but if we die without Christ, we experience eternal death.

We all suffer the **consequences of the fall of man**. Our salvation is in calling upon the name of the Lord and trusting in Jesus' perfect sacrifice for our sin. When Jesus comes for all those who have trusted in Him, God will restore all things. He will create a new heaven and a new earth to replace that which sin destroyed. Mankind will no longer be "fallen" but restored and redeemed by the blood of the Lamb of God.

GOD'S GRACE, MERCY AND LOVE

In the Garden God was faithful by speaking, promising, providing, and cursing. Right away, we see that this is still a story about love. There is good news in the garden: the good news that God is still God and He has not given up on His plans, His purposes, and His people. He is still a God of glory and grace.

That is good news indeed. After Adam and Eve sinned, they discovered something they hadn't noticed before: they were naked. God made garments of skins for them; this is significant in three ways.

First, this is the first redemptive step done by God, which we can link to how Christ's righteousness clothes us. Second, a life was sacrificed to make these clothes. We can link that to Christ's sacrifice.

And third, God dressed them, a mark of acceptance similar to how the father clothed the prodigal son with a new robe when he returned home.

Unfortunately, God had to drive them out from the perfect garden to keep them away from the tree of life, preventing them from living forever in sin. God placed angelic guards with flaming swords turning every which way to shield the way from man.

The physical approach to eternal life has been completely cut off. The only way is through Jesus. This was a demonstration of God's love for us. God is love and just. God is holy, and we are sinful; there must be separation. But God's love is shown through these redemptive activities despite human disobedience and fallen nature. God fixing clothes for them, and even sending Jesus to die on the cross to redeem undeserving people illustration of love.

Let's visit back to Genesis 3:15 when God spoke to the spiritual serpent; Satan. "And I will put enmity between thee and the woman, and between thy seed and her seed; it shall bruise thy head, and thou shalt bruise his heel."

Here is the very first prophecy of the death and resurrection of Jesus Christ. Whether the man and woman understood, they had just heard in God's curse on the serpent/Satan the plan to restore what had been lost by their betrayal and rebellion against their creator. It establishes the parameters by which God will redeem His people from their sin.

From the earliest times, **Genesis 3:15** has been called the proto-evangelium because it is the first note of God's redemptive intention following the fall in the garden of Eden. When Adam and Eve failed to obey the terms of the covenant of works, God did not destroy them (which would have served justice), but instead revealed His covenant of grace to them by promising a Savior, one who would restore the kingdom that had latterly been destroyed.

God's method of grace is costly: the heel of the Savior will be bruised. Evidently, this is a metaphor that in the context is to be contrasted with the blow the serpent receives (the crushing of his head), but it is immediately apparent what this involves—the shedding of substitutionary blood.

That seems to be what lies behind the provision of animal skins as a covering for Adam and Eve. Blood needs to be shed for sin to be forgiven, perhaps this accounts for why it is that Abel's offering (the firstborn of his flock) is accepted but Cain's (the fruits of the soil) is not.

The way is now clear: "without the shedding of blood there is no forgiveness of sins". Genesis 3:1 introduces Satan in the Bible, and while he is not on every page, he has a leading role. He is called the destroyer, the enemy, the father of lies, a murderer, the evil one and many other things. The Bible also says he is crafty.

Other translations include sneaky, clever, cunning, subtle, intelligent and shrewd. Satan is a clever devil who is good at what he does. If you lived a thousand years, you could easily become an expert at something: music, math, logic, drama or any number of things. Satan has been around longer than that, and has refined his craft to an art form. He is so skillful, in fact, that he leads the whole world astray, wrote John.

We know how to split the atom and launch rockets, but after thousands of years, because of Satan's influence, there is still no consensus on who God is, what He requires, or if He even exists. Satan is God's enemy, but he cannot attack God directly, so he attacks those made in God's image, and dearly loved by Him. Satan knows his doom is certain, and wants to bring as many people down with him as he can.

Our enemy, the devil prowls around looking to see who he can destroy. He hates humankind and, while beaten at the cross, has but a little time left to wage war on God's children. Since the life and death of Christ, the only power left to him is through lies and deceit.

THE GIFT OF GOD

This gift of eternal life is the remedy to the sin that we are born with. It is the cure-all prescribed for us by the Great Physician who donated it Himself through the shedding of His blood on the cross.

So, no matter what happens in this life, we can praise God for His faithfulness instead of worrying about our frailty, knowing that when God does allow us to die, we will be "translated" into the next life where there is no more "death… nor mourning, nor crying, nor pain anymore, for the former things have passed away" (**Revelation 21:4**, ESV). Eternal life is also knowing God, intimately. Knowing the only True and Living God means having a personal relationship with Him - not just knowing about Him.

God's presence in our lives produces peace, purpose and power. Peace shows itself by the ability to properly relate to God, other persons, ourselves and our world. This shows itself through loving relationships. You seek with God's help to love Him with all your heart and love your neighbor as yourself. Purpose provides understanding of God's desires for our lives. The power of God is "able to keep you from stumbling, and to make you stand in the presence of His glory blameless with great joy." (Jude 24) Power is also the ability to do all we were put in this world to accomplish.

Jesus shed his blood on the cross so that man could be forgiven and cleansed from sin. (Hebrews 9:22) "And according to the law almost all things are purified with blood, and without shedding of blood there is no remission (forgiveness).

One has to exercise faith in what Jesus did for man on the cross in order to receive the gift of God which is eternal life. In Ephesians 2:8-9 we read "For by grace you have been saved through faith, and that not of yourselves; it is the gift of God, not of works, lest anyone should boast.'

Jesus Christ is the medium through which God imparts salvation and the bridge that God uses to connect us. This means that when we receive Jesus, we get this gift. Eternal life can never be purchased in any way, it is entirely a free gift. The cost of this gift is the death of the Savior, Jesus Christ. The gift of eternal life is available to anyone who, after recognizing his own sinfulness, places his or her personal faith in Jesus Christ as the only Savior.

Sin is disobedience. Disobedience is doing what God says is wrong - in act, attitude or thought. "Anyone who hates his brother is a murderer" (I John 3:15). "Anyone who looks ... lustfully has already committed adultery in his heart" (Matthew 5:28). God requires perfection. Jesus said: "Be perfect . . . as your heavenly Father is perfect" (Matthew 5:48).

Sin separates us from God and damages our ability to relate to people. "Your iniquities have separated you from your God" (Isa. 59:2). God must now relate to us as our righteous Judge instead of our loving father.

When we are not rightly related to God, our ability to properly relate to people is damaged also. We hurt each other. We especially hurt ourselves. We grieve God by disobeying His laws. The only answer to this problem is Jesus.

Jesus is the mediator. "There is one God and one mediator between God and men, the man Christ Jesus, who gave himself as a ransom for all men" (I Tim. 2:5-6). Not only is He true man, He is also true God.

The prophet Isaiah, looking forward to His birth 800 years before it happened said: "To us a child is born, to us a son is given and he will be called Mighty God" (Isa. 9:6). As True God He has equal dignity with God and His payment for man's sin had infinite value.

As True Man, He had perfect sympathy with man and can pay for man's sins. He did everything necessary to restore relationships. He lived the perfect life. The apostle Peter declared, "He committed no sin, and no deceit was found in His mouth" (I Peter 2:22).

Jesus died for us. "He himself bore our sins in His body on the tree, so that we might die to sins and live for righteousness" (I Peter 2:24). "He forgave all your sins, and blotted out the charges proved against you. He took this list of sins and destroyed it by nailing it to Christ's Cross" (Col. 2:13,14).

Miraculously, He came out of the grave alive. Luke declared: "He showed himself to these men (the Apostles) and gave many convincing proofs that He was alive. He appeared to them over a period of forty days" (Acts 1:3). This is the most important and one of the best attested facts of history. Now it is possible to receive eternal life.

When you receive a restored relationship, your mindset must change. Changing your mind is not being sorry for getting caught. Changing your mind is being sorry for doing wrong, turning from it with God's help and desiring Jesus as Lord. "He who conceals his sins does not prosper, but whoever confesses and renounces them finds mercy" (Proverbs 28:13).

Changing your mind about doing wrong is necessary! God's holy nature will not allow Him to forgive sin without it. But to be sorry for past wrong cannot undo it. The relationship is restored through faith.

Faith is not mere blind belief. It is not a blind leap in the dark. It is based on the promises of the Bible that have actually happened in history; the facts that Jesus lived a perfect life, died and then came out of the grave alive.

After Jesus returned from the dead He said to Thomas, "Reach out your hand, and put it into my side; and stop doubting and believe." Thomas answered and said to him, "My Lord and my God!" (John 20:27,28) Faith is not mere head belief. Only knowing about food in the mind will not satisfy hunger. It must be eaten. Simply knowing about Jesus in the mind is not the same as having an intimate, personal relationship with Him. Faith is not mere now belief.

Jesus taught us to depend on God for needs in the daily life. He urged us to pray, "Give us today our daily bread" (Matthew 6:11). But there is more to life than things that are seen:

"What is seen is temporary, but what is unseen is eternal" (II Cor. 4:18). Faith is relying on Jesus Christ alone for your eternal life.nThe apostle John said, "God so loved the world, that He gave His one and only Son, that whoever believes in Him shall not perish but have eternal life" (John 3:16). Jesus said: "No one comes to the Father except through Me"

(John 14:6). Faith is not belief without evidence, but it is a commitment to Jesus Christ without reservation. This is the most important decision you will ever make in your life.

Are you ready to receive Eternal Life? Express your trust in Christ by sincerely praying the following and God will give you eternal life.

Lord Jesus, for too long I've kept you out of my life. I know that I am a sinner and that I cannot save myself. No longer will I close the door when I hear you knocking. By faith I gratefully receive your gift of salvation. I am ready to trust you as my Lord and Savior. Thank you, Lord Jesus, for coming to earth. I believe you are the Son of God who died on the cross for my sins and rose from the dead on the third day. Thank you for bearing my sins and giving me the gift of eternal life. I believe your words are true. Come into my heart, Lord Jesus, and be my Savior. Amen.

Now that you have received the gift of eternal life, God and the heavens are rejoicing. Your life has been renewed.

For if a man belongs to Christ, he is a new person. The old life is gone. New life has begun. (2 Corinthians 5:17)

REFERENCES

https://www.biblestudytools.com/msg/
colossians/passage/?q=colossians+1:16-17

https://www.crosswalk.com/faith/spiritual-life/10-ways-
god-is-the-perfect-father-in-case-yours-wasn-t.html

https://desirejesus.com/blog/2018/6/26/god-the-son

https://www.biblestudytools.com/
dictionary/son-of-god-the/

https://www.biblestudytools.com/bible-study/topical-
studies/proofs-that-jesus-is-the-son-of-god.html

https://learn.gcs.edu/mod/book/view.
php?id=5609&chapterid=396

https://www.biblword.net/
how-can-jesus-be-god-and-son-of-god-at-the-same-time/

https://www.google.com/search?q=Hebrews+1%3A3&oq=
Hebrews+1%3A3&aqs=chrome..69i57.7047j0j7&sourceid
=chrome&ie=UTF-8

https://www.google.com/search?q=philippians+2&oq=
Ph&aqs=chrome.3.69i57j0i67l4j69i60l3.5232j0j7&
sourceid=chrome&ie=UTF-8

https://www.crosswalk.com/faith/bible-study/why-
does-jesus-ask-who-do-you-say-i-am.html

https://www.trussvilletribune.com/2019/08/01/kids-talk-
about-god-why-does-the-bible-call-jesus-the-word/

https://theologyforwomen.org/2010/04/her-
desire-will-be-for-her-husband.html

https://www.gotquestions.org/fall-affect-humanity.html

https://www.christianity.com/wiki/salvation/
mean-that-the-gift-of-god-is-eternal-life.html

http://www.csun.edu/reformed/docs/eternal_life.htm

https://biblesfortheworld.org/is-satan-rea
l/?gclid=CjwKCAiAvaGRBhBlEiwAiY-
yMBaxkSULDd1VrwRNv8g-NShsa_muGDZ-
asYw7F82BLJDNAmqCN0yNhoCcHwQAvD_BwE